About the Editor

Born in Mexico, Glen Alberto Salazar grew up in California. He has taken Japanese language classes in college and holds a bachelor's degree in French language and literature from the University of California at Berkeley. In addition to writing, he enjoys Japanese cuisine, art, and pop culture. He currently lives in Northern California.

Also by Glen Alberto Salazar

Pistachio the Squirrel (children's book)

Le petit nomade/The Little Nomad
(bilingual short story in Berkeley's
Vagabond)

A Little Book Of
Haiku

Glen Alberto Salazar

Splendor Books

CreateSpace ISBN-13: 978-1479190270
CreateSpace ISBN-10: 1479190276

Book design by Glen Alberto Salazar

Printed in the United States of America
10 9 8 7 6 5 4 3 2 1

For Okazaki Sensei, who taught me
Japanese at the Santa Rosa Junior College.
ありがとう ございました。

Contents

Introduction

This is a little book about haiku, brief Japanese poems that have universal appeal. Haiku capture vivid snapshots of life and nature in their simple form and content. From childhood to adulthood, haiku poetry can be taught at any age. The world of haiku is a real treat full of wonder, humor and adventure.

While haiku was born in the 17th century, its soul can be traced back to the poetic tradition that preceded it by a thousand years. From the 8th to the 11th centuries, early Japanese poetry illustrated joyful images of nature, drawing inspiration from the Shinto belief on nature spirits and deities. Nonetheless some early poems were written with melancholy or nostalgia, revealing the poet's perceptions and emotions.

From the 8th to 13th centuries, medieval Japanese poetry concerned itself with the theme of love. These medieval poems expressed sadness in the transience of life, thus showing influence from the Buddhist doctrine of impermanence. Zen Buddhism would later give haiku its meditative soul.

Inspired by Classical Chinese poetry, early and medieval Japanese poems were known as *waka*, meaning "Japanese poem or song." *Waka* were subdivided into two main types: *choka* and *tanka*. *Choka* was a long form of *waka, while tanka* was a short form. *Tanka* became Japan's most popular poetic expression from which haiku developed. *Tanka* was strictly written using 31 syllables (*on*) in a 5–7–5–7–7 pattern.

During the 16th and 17th centuries, *renga* appeared as a reaction against the classical *tanka*. *Renga* were composed in a language using common speech, slang and Mandarin words. Then, *haikai* emerged as radical poetic verses. Haikai used comic and inelegant subject matter to mock everyday life – sex, money, domestic life, etc.

Renga were 31 syllable (*on*) *tankas*. The opening and closing parts were comprised of 17 and 14 syllable (*on*) stanzas respectively. The opening verse was called *hokku* (related to *haikai*), it was usually written by the master poet. The opening *hokku* of a *renga* became the most important verse and it eventually led to the recognition of *hokku* as a poetic form in its own right. In the 17th century, Bashō wrote the first haiku. In the late 19th century, Shiki invented the word *haiku* to describe an independent hokku.

Before 1900, Japanese haiku were usually written using 17 syllables (*on*) in a 5-7-5 pattern, a "cutting word" (*kireji*) that cuts a haiku into two images or ideas, and a seasonal marker (*kigo*). Since then, free-verse haiku have experimented with the traditional pattern of syllables (*on*), while others have omitted their seasonal markers (*kigo*).

In general, modern haiku written in other languages break the 5-7-5 syllables (*on*) rule. For example while the rhythm of

Japanese poems emphasizes syllables (*on*), the rhythm of English poems emphasizes stress. So, haiku can be written in fewer syllables (*on*) in English, than in Japanese.

Senryū is a friend of haiku, named after *haikai* poet Senryū Karai who popularized the genre in the 18th century. Like modern haiku, *senryū* loosely follow the 5–7–5 syllabic (*on*) pattern. Unlike haiku, *senryū* don't have a cutting word (*kireji*) or a seasonal marker (*kigo*). Essential to *senryū* is humor (*okashimi*) that deals with human foibles, a minor weakness or failing of character. *Senryū* is written with lightness (karumi), which means the ability to produce cynical and dark humor out of common things or people, or the ability to laugh at oneself. *Senryū* is also written with "insightful information" (*ugachi*) into human nature.

Zappai is another friend of haiku. Like haiku and *senryū*, *zappai* is a brief poem written with 17 syllables (*on*). Nevertheless, it doesn't follow the other rules that give haiku or *senryū* their essence.

   This short anthology is intended to be a light introduction to 100 classical haiku. The first four chapters present the haiku from the four most beloved and revered haiku masters: Bashō, Buson, Issa, and Shiki. These first four chapters are arranged chronologically according to the time period in which the haiku masters lived. The last chapter presents the haiku of Chiyo-ni, who is placed last, in order to emphasize the underrepresentation of female haiku writers in old Japan. In summary, haiku provide children and adults with hidden insights into nature and life through poetic meditation.

Chapter 1

Matsuo Bashō
(1644–1694)

An old pond–
A frog jumps in
The sound of water.

Winter shower–
Even the monkey seems to want
A little coat of straw.

Temple bells die out
The fragrant blossoms remain
A perfect evening!

The wind from Mt. Fuji
I've brought on my fan
A gift from Edo.*

From all directions
Winds bring petals of cherry
Into the grebe lake.

* Edo is the old name for Tokyo.

The butterfly is perfuming
It's wings in the scent
Of the orchid.

Sleep on horseback,
The far moon in a continuing dream,
Stream of roasting tea.

A monk sips morning tea,
It's quiet,
The chrysanthemum's flowering.

A wild sea–
In the distance over Sado*
The Milky Way.

Wont you come and see
Loneliness? Just one leaf
From the kiri tree.

Heard, not seen
The camellia poured rainwater
When it leaned.

* Sado is an island located in the Chūbu
  region of Japan.

A caterpillar
This deep into fall
Still not a butterfly.

Autumn moonlight–
A worm digs silently
Into the chestnut.

Dying cricket,
How he sings out
His life.

Mii temple–
Knocking on the gate for a wish
Today's moon.

Lonely silence–
A single cicada's cry
Sinking into stone.

Traveling this high
Mountain trail, delighted
By violets.

The bee emerging
From deep within the peony
Departs reluctantly.

The shallows–
A crane's thighs splashed
In cool waves.

Blue seas
Breaking waves smell of rice wine
Tonight's moon.

Chapter 2

Yosa Buson
(1716–1783)

Blow of an ax
Pine scent
The Winter woods.

Morning fog-
The road full of people
From a painter's dream.

The first frost–
Seeing a suffering crane
In the distance.

Calligraphy* of geese
Against the sky–
The moon seals it.

A whale
Down it goes, and more and more
Up goes its tail.

* A script of high aesthetic value made with a
  brush and ink, especially that of Chinese,
  Japanese, and Korean.

At a roadside shrine,
Before a stony Buddha
A firefly burns.

Mushroom hunting–
Raising my head
The moon over the peak.

A kite floats
At the place in the sky
Where it floated yesterday.

The blossoming pear–
A woman reads a letter
In the moonlight.

Waterfowls–
One lantern comes out
Of the castle.

The old man
Cutting barley–
Bent like a sickle.

Sparrow singing—
Its tiny mouth
Open.

A bat flits
In moonlight
Above the plum blossoms.

They end their flight
One by one—
Crows at dusk.

Listening to the moon,
Gazing at the croaking of frogs
In a field of ripe rice.

Before the white chrysanthemum
The scissors hesitate
A moment.

A day slow in going
Echoes
In the corner of Kyoto.

More than last year,
I now feel solitude;
Autumn twilight.

Old well–
Leaping for a mosquito
A dark fish sound.

Plum blossoms in bloom,
In Kitano teahouse,
The master of sumo.*

* Sumo is a Japanese form of wrestling.

Chapter 3

Kobayashi Issa
(1763–1827)

In my deserted home village
The old cherry tree
Now in bloom.

A faint yellow rose
Almost hidden in deep grass
And then it moves.

Summer night–
Even the stars
Are whispering to each other.

Don't kill that fly!
It is making a prayer to you
By rubbing its hands and feet.

Even wild roses
Of a downtrodden land
Reach enlightenment.

The distant mountains
Are reflected in the eye
Of a dragonfly.

The old hand
Swats a fly–
Already gone.

Great Japan–
Where a bird sings
The lotus sutra.*

* A sutra is a scripture that records the oral
  teachings of the Buddha.

O snail
Climb Mt. Fuji,
But slowly, slowly!

Two houses–
Two people making mochi,*
Autumn rain.

A nightboat
Sails away–
Iluminated by wildfire.

* Mochi is a sweet Japanese rice cake made of
  glutinous rice.

The dragonfly
Dressed in red
Off to the festival.

First Kimono*–
May you quickly grow to
A naughty age.

My noontime nap–
Disrupted by people singing
Rice–planting songs.

  * A kimono is a traditional Japanese garment
    worn mostly by women.

Grasshopper–
Do not trample to pieces
The pearls of bright dew.

House burnt down–
Fleas
Dance in embers.

O owl!
Make some other face.
This is spring rain.

A flowering plum
And a nightingale's love song
He remains alone.

Red morning sky,
Snail;
Are you glad of it?

Blossoms at night,
And the faces of people
Moved by music.

Chapter 4

Masaoka Shiki
(1867–1902)

In the coolness
Gods and Buddhas
Dwell as neighbors.

Evening snow falling,
A pair of mandarin ducks
On an ancient lake.

Lotus leaves in a pond
Ride on water
Rain in June.

A carp leaps up
Crinkling
The autumn moonlight.

Red dragonfly
In the sky of Tsukuba*
No cloud.

* Tsukuba is a sacred mountain located in the
  Kantō region of Japan.

Paper dolls–
Their faces look like
They want to be in love.

A cock crows
At the foot of the small Mt. Fuji
Peach blossoms.

Fanning out its tail
In the spring breeze,
See–a peacock.

My fate
Fortune tells–
Autumn winds.

Stillness–
Fireflies are glowing over
Deep water.

Moon at twilight
A cluster of petals falling
From the cherry tree.

Hometown–
Festivals are over
Flavorful persimmons.

Weary of reading
I go into a field–
A hazy field.

After the battle
A pear tree blooms
By the ruined house.

Behind the strand
Of winter trees–
A red sunset.

Rice reaping–
No smoke rising from
The cremation ground today.

How cool it is!
A small crab, in the rain,
Climbs on a pine.

In cleft on cleft,
On rock face after rock face–
Wild azaleas.

Pruning a rose
Sounds of scissors
On a bright May day.

Midday sun–
Sunglasses on my scarecrow
Just for fun.

Chapter 5

Fukuda Chiyo-ni
(1703–1775)

It's play for the cranes
Flying up to the clouds
The year's first sunrise.

Tea flowers–
Their blooming
Delays the dusk.

Staring
At my snow-white reflection
In the water.

Over the flowing water
Chasing its shadow–
The dragonfly.

The coolness–
On the bottom of her Kimono*
In the bamboo grove.

* A kimono is a traditional Japanese garment
  worn mostly by women.

Moonflower–
The beauty
Of hidden things.

Stars' meeting
Which one
Speaks first.

Moonlit night–
Out on the stone
A cricket singing.

A dandelion
Now and then interrupting
The butterfly's dream.

Each sound of
The temple bell is different
In the wind.

Morning glory!
The well bucket–entangled,
I ask for water.

Fishing rod–
Its line brushed
By the summer moon.

Rouged lips
Forgotten–
Clear spring water.

Moonflowers–
When a woman's skin
Is revealed.

Dawn's separation—
Unknown
To dolls.

Woman's desire
Deeply rooted—
The wild violets.

Green grass—
Between the blades
The color of water.

To tangle
Or untangle the willow-
Its up to the wind.

Just for today
Using men
For rice planting.

Spring rain-
All things on earth
Become beautiful.

Conclusion

Now, as you can see, the art of haiku gives us hidden insights into nature and everyday life. While going through an uncertain and sometimes confusing world, haiku provide a way to stand back and reflect on it all. By learning from the masters and meditating on their haiku, we can gain a more enlightened view of life.

The world of haiku should not only be explored by children, but also by adults. There is so much to learn from haiku, and from its friends (*senryū* and *zappai*), that it would take more than a lifetime to learn. The next step to take in this adventure would be to start writing your own haiku.

Observe! Meditate! Create! That is the spirit of haiku!

Taking It Further

Haiku Journals

Once you have a chance to write your own haiku, you should consider submitting your work to the following haiku journals for publication:

Frogpond
http://www.hsa-haiku.org/frogpond/index.html

Modern Haiku
http://www.modernhaiku.org/

Roadrunner
http://www.roadrunnerjournal.net/

Senryū Journal

For those of you who write senryū, you can submit your work to the following senryū journal and with a little luck have your work published:

Prune Juice
http://prunejuice.wordpress.com/

Japanese Culture

For those of you who wish to know more about Japanese culture, then a good place to start would be the Japan Foundation. As a cultural institution, the Japan Foundation promotes Japanese arts and culture, Japanese language education, and Japanese studies and exchange programs. It is headquartered in Tokyo, with branches around the world. The Japan Foundation website is:

http://www.jpf.go.jp/

JAPANFOUNDATION

Further Reading

Gurga, Lee. *Haiku: A Poet's Guide*. Lincoln, Illinois: Modern Haiku Press, 2003. Print

Yasuda, Kenneth. *The Japanese Haiku: Its Essential Nature and History*. Boston, Massachusetts: Tuttle Publishing, 2002. Print.

Index

Made in the USA
Middletown, DE
18 November 2016